RESTAURANT

REVIEWING

Dee Adams

This Book Belongs to

_____

Disclaimer

Companies or individuals referenced in this book did not pay for any mentions. Inclusion of any companies or services in this book does not imply endorsement by the author.

The opinions expressed are solely those of Dee Adams.

Always consult a qualified experienced legal professional for your specific situation.

How to Use This Book

Back in the early to mid-1990s, class action lawsuits led to fifty-eight million dollars won in federal cases on behalf of African American patrons discriminated against in restaurants for denial of seating, requiring payment in advance, or ushering diners to sit in the back of the restaurant.

According to the website Legal Watch, it was to be the end of racism toward patrons of color in the American diner industry.

So, what happened?

In today's world, rude or discriminatory treatment is experienced too often by African Americans while dining out, with and without friends or family present. Other groups as well experience ill treatment, whether because of ethnicity or occupation (such as police officers refused service because of their weapons).

When is poor treatment in a restaurant considered poor service, bad management practice, or discrimination?

As an individual or group project, this notebook can be used to record a good or questionable dining experience. More than 25 questions and reference sources will help you focus on the service received (or lack thereof) by using the pages provided. And related informative articles and related laws for seven states are included in the appendix.

Opening a restaurant has always headed the list of favorite startups for aspiring business owners. It's a popular entrepreneurial theme on countless sitcoms, crime dramas, and movies.

The restaurant industry is complex. Many diners of all races enjoy good dining experiences. But some diners file lawsuits.

Use this book to help you document your experiences with restaurants and other food services.

The following pages feature the questions you should be asking yourself as you reflect on your dining experiences, whether good or bad.

My Dining Experience

Name and address of the restaurant:

Date visited:

Arrival time:

Number in party:

How did you find out about this restaurant?

What is the history of this restaurant?

Who owns the restaurant?

How were you greeted at the door?

How long was the wait to be seated?

Did you like the location of your seating? Why or why not?

Did you like your waitperson? Why or why not?

How long did it take to get a menu?

How long did it take for the food to arrive?

How was the food?

Were there food handling issues? Describe:

What was the attitude of the workers who waited on your table?

What was the overall attitude of the staff toward you and other diners?

Were restaurant workers a diverse group? E.g., host, hostess, waiters, waitresses, busboys, chef/cook.

Were restaurant patrons a diverse group? If yes, how so?
Race, age, gender?

What did you like most about your visit?

What did you like least about your visit?

How would you have improved your dining experience?

Describe any incident (Who, What, Where, When, Why):

Did you feel singled out for poor treatment? How so?

Did you notice others receiving the same treatment?

Did you notice others **did not** receive the same poor treatment?

Tipping: If applicable, did you consider asking for the manager before departure and explaining why you did not tip or why you left a reduced tip? What is the standard tip for your part of the country?

What is the restaurant's reputation in the community?

My Dining Experience

Name and address of the restaurant:

Date visited:

Arrival time:

Number in party:

How did you find out about this restaurant?

What is the history of this restaurant?

Who owns the restaurant?

How were you greeted at the door?

How long was the wait to be seated?

Did you like the location of your seating? Why or why not?

Did you like your waitperson? Why or why not?

How long did it take to get a menu?

How long did it take for the food to arrive?

How was the food?

Were there food handling issues? Describe:

What was the attitude of the workers who waited on your table?

What was the overall attitude of the staff toward you and other diners?

Were restaurant workers a diverse group? E.g., host, hostess, waiters, waitresses, busboys, chef/cook.

Were restaurant patrons a diverse group? If yes, how so? Race, age, gender?

What did you like most about your visit?

What did you like least about your visit?

How would you have improved your dining experience?

Describe any incident (Who, What, Where, When, Why):

Did you feel singled out for poor treatment? How so?

Did you notice others receiving the same treatment?

Did you notice others **did not** receive the same poor treatment?

Tipping: If applicable, did you consider asking for the manager before departure and explaining why you did not tip or why you left a reduced tip? What is the standard tip for your part of the country?

What is the restaurant's reputation in the community?

My Dining Experience

Name and address of the restaurant:

Date visited:

Arrival time:

Number in party:

How did you find out about this restaurant?

What is the history of this restaurant?

Who owns the restaurant?

How were you greeted at the door?

How long was the wait to be seated?

Did you like the location of your seating? Why or why not?

Did you like your waitperson? Why or why not?

How long did it take to get a menu?

How long did it take for the food to arrive?

How was the food?

Were there food handling issues? Describe:

What was the attitude of the workers who waited on your table?

What was the overall attitude of the staff toward you and other diners?

Were restaurant workers a diverse group? E.g., host, hostess, waiters, waitresses, busboys, chef/cook.

Were restaurant patrons a diverse group? If yes, how so?
Race, age, gender?

What did you like most about your visit?

What did you like least about your visit?

How would you have improved your dining experience?

Describe any incident (Who, What, Where, When, Why):

Did you feel singled out for poor treatment? How so?

Did you notice others receiving the same treatment?

Did you notice others **did not** receive the same poor treatment?

Tipping: If applicable, did you consider asking for the manager before departure and explaining why you did not tip or why you left a reduced tip? What is the standard tip for your part of the country?

What is the restaurant's reputation in the community?

My Dining Experience

Name and address of the restaurant:

Date visited:

Arrival time:

Number in party:

How did you find out about this restaurant?

What is the history of this restaurant?

Who owns the restaurant?

How were you greeted at the door?

How long was the wait to be seated?

Did you like the location of your seating? Why or why not?

Did you like your waitperson? Why or why not?

How long did it take to get a menu?

How long did it take for the food to arrive?

How was the food?

Were there food handling issues? Describe:

What was the attitude of the workers who waited on your table?

What was the overall attitude of the staff toward you and other diners?

Were restaurant workers a diverse group? E.g., host, hostess, waiters, waitresses, busboys, chef/cook.

Were restaurant patrons a diverse group? If yes, how so?
Race, age, gender?

What did you like most about your visit?

What did you like least about your visit?

How would you have improved your dining experience?

Describe any incident (Who, What, Where, When, Why):

Did you feel singled out for poor treatment? How so?

Did you notice others receiving the same treatment?

Did you notice others **did not** receive the same poor treatment?

Tipping: If applicable, did you consider asking for the manager before departure and explaining why you did not tip or why you left a reduced tip? What is the standard tip for your part of the country?

What is the restaurant's reputation in the community?

My Dining Experience

Name and address of the restaurant:

Date visited:

Arrival time:

Number in party:

How did you find out about this restaurant?

What is the history of this restaurant?

Who owns the restaurant?

How were you greeted at the door?

How long was the wait to be seated?

Did you like the location of your seating? Why or why not?

Did you like your waitperson? Why or why not?

How long did it take to get a menu?

How long did it take for the food to arrive?

How was the food?

Were there food handling issues? Describe:

What was the attitude of the workers who waited on your table?

What was the overall attitude of the staff toward you and other diners?

Were restaurant workers a diverse group? E.g., host, hostess, waiters, waitresses, busboys, chef/cook.

Were restaurant patrons a diverse group? If yes, how so? Race, age, gender?

What did you like most about your visit?

What did you like least about your visit?

How would you have improved your dining experience?

Describe any incident (Who, What, Where, When, Why):

Did you feel singled out for poor treatment? How so?

Did you notice others receiving the same treatment?

Did you notice others **did not** receive the same poor treatment?

Tipping: If applicable, did you consider asking for the manager before departure and explaining why you did not tip or why you left a reduced tip? What is the standard tip for your part of the country?

What is the restaurant's reputation in the community?

My Dining Experience

Name and address of the restaurant:

Date visited:

Arrival time:

Number in party:

How did you find out about this restaurant?

What is the history of this restaurant?

Who owns the restaurant?

How were you greeted at the door?

How long was the wait to be seated?

Did you like the location of your seating? Why or why not?

Did you like your waitperson? Why or why not?

How long did it take to get a menu?

How long did it take for the food to arrive?

How was the food?

Were there food handling issues? Describe:

What was the attitude of the workers who waited on your table?

What was the overall attitude of the staff toward you and other diners?

Were restaurant workers a diverse group? E.g., host, hostess, waiters, waitresses, busboys, chef/cook.

Were restaurant patrons a diverse group? If yes, how so?
Race, age, gender?

What did you like most about your visit?

What did you like least about your visit?

How would you have improved your dining experience?

Describe any incident (Who, What, Where, When, Why):

Did you feel singled out for poor treatment? How so?

Did you notice others receiving the same treatment?

Did you notice others **did not** receive the same poor treatment?

Tipping: If applicable, did you consider asking for the manager before departure and explaining why you did not tip or why you left a reduced tip? What is the standard tip for your part of the country?

What is the restaurant's reputation in the community?

My Dining Experience

Name and address of the restaurant:

Date visited:

Arrival time:

Number in party:

How did you find out about this restaurant?

What is the history of this restaurant?

Who owns the restaurant?

How were you greeted at the door?

How long was the wait to be seated?

Did you like the location of your seating? Why or why not?

Did you like your waitperson? Why or why not?

How long did it take to get a menu?

How long did it take for the food to arrive?

How was the food?

Were there food handling issues? Describe:

What was the attitude of the workers who waited on your table?

What was the overall attitude of the staff toward you and other diners?

Were restaurant workers a diverse group? E.g., host, hostess, waiters, waitresses, busboys, chef/cook.

Were restaurant patrons a diverse group? If yes, how so?
Race, age, gender?

What did you like most about your visit?

What did you like least about your visit?

How would you have improved your dining experience?

Describe any incident (Who, What, Where, When, Why):

Did you feel singled out for poor treatment? How so?

Did you notice others receiving the same treatment?

Did you notice others **did not** receive the same poor treatment?

Tipping: If applicable, did you consider asking for the manager before departure and explaining why you did not tip or why you left a reduced tip? What is the standard tip for your part of the country?

What is the restaurant's reputation in the community?

My Dining Experience

Name and address of the restaurant:

Date visited:

Arrival time:

Number in party:

How did you find out about this restaurant?

What is the history of this restaurant?

Who owns the restaurant?

How were you greeted at the door?

How long was the wait to be seated?

Did you like the location of your seating? Why or why not?

Did you like your waitperson? Why or why not?

How long did it take to get a menu?

How long did it take for the food to arrive?

How was the food?

Were there food handling issues? Describe:

What was the attitude of the workers who waited on your table?

What was the overall attitude of the staff toward you and other diners?

Were restaurant workers a diverse group? E.g., host, hostess, waiters, waitresses, busboys, chef/cook.

Were restaurant patrons a diverse group? If yes, how so?
Race, age, gender?

What did you like most about your visit?

What did you like least about your visit?

How would you have improved your dining experience?

Describe any incident (Who, What, Where, When, Why):

Did you feel singled out for poor treatment? How so?

Did you notice others receiving the same treatment?

Did you notice others **did not** receive the same poor treatment?

Tipping: If applicable, did you consider asking for the manager before departure and explaining why you did not tip or why you left a reduced tip? What is the standard tip for your part of the country?

What is the restaurant's reputation in the community?

My Dining Experience

Name and address of the restaurant:

Date visited:

Arrival time:

Number in party:

How did you find out about this restaurant?

What is the history of this restaurant?

Who owns the restaurant?

How were you greeted at the door?

How long was the wait to be seated?

Did you like the location of your seating? Why or why not?

Did you like your waitperson? Why or why not?

How long did it take to get a menu?

How long did it take for the food to arrive?

How was the food?

Were there food handling issues? Describe:

What was the attitude of the workers who waited on your table?

What was the overall attitude of the staff toward you and other diners?

Were restaurant workers a diverse group? E.g., host, hostess, waiters, waitresses, busboys, chef/cook.

Were restaurant patrons a diverse group? If yes, how so?
Race, age, gender?

What did you like most about your visit?

What did you like least about your visit?

How would you have improved your dining experience?

Describe any incident (Who, What, Where, When, Why):

Did you feel singled out for poor treatment? How so?

Did you notice others receiving the same treatment?

Did you notice others **did not** receive the same poor treatment?

Tipping: If applicable, did you consider asking for the manager before departure and explaining why you did not tip or why you left a reduced tip? What is the standard tip for your part of the country?

What is the restaurant's reputation in the community?

My Dining Experience

Name and address of the restaurant:

Date visited:

Arrival time:

Number in party:

How did you find out about this restaurant?

What is the history of this restaurant?

Who owns the restaurant?

How were you greeted at the door?

How long was the wait to be seated?

Did you like the location of your seating? Why or why not?

Did you like your waitperson? Why or why not?

How long did it take to get a menu?

How long did it take for the food to arrive?

How was the food?

Were there food handling issues? Describe:

What was the attitude of the workers who waited on your table?

What was the overall attitude of the staff toward you and other diners?

Were restaurant workers a diverse group? E.g., host, hostess, waiters, waitresses, busboys, chef/cook.

Were restaurant patrons a diverse group? If yes, how so?
Race, age, gender?

What did you like most about your visit?

What did you like least about your visit?

How would you have improved your dining experience?

Describe any incident (Who, What, Where, When, Why):

Did you feel singled out for poor treatment? How so?

Did you notice others receiving the same treatment?

Did you notice others **did not** receive the same poor treatment?

Tipping: If applicable, did you consider asking for the manager before departure and explaining why you did not tip or why you left a reduced tip? What is the standard tip for your part of the country?

What is the restaurant's reputation in the community?

My Dining Experience

Name and address of the restaurant:

Date visited:

Arrival time:

Number in party:

How did you find out about this restaurant?

What is the history of this restaurant?

Who owns the restaurant?

How were you greeted at the door?

How long was the wait to be seated?

Did you like the location of your seating? Why or why not?

Did you like your waitperson? Why or why not?

How long did it take to get a menu?

How long did it take for the food to arrive?

How was the food?

Were there food handling issues? Describe:

What was the attitude of the workers who waited on your table?

What was the overall attitude of the staff toward you and other diners?

Were restaurant workers a diverse group? E.g., host, hostess, waiters, waitresses, busboys, chef/cook.

Were restaurant patrons a diverse group? If yes, how so?
Race, age, gender?

What did you like most about your visit?

What did you like least about your visit?

How would you have improved your dining experience?

Describe any incident (Who, What, Where, When, Why):

Did you feel singled out for poor treatment? How so?

Did you notice others receiving the same treatment?

Did you notice others **did not** receive the same poor treatment?

Tipping: If applicable, did you consider asking for the manager before departure and explaining why you did not tip or why you left a reduced tip? What is the standard tip for your part of the country?

What is the restaurant's reputation in the community?

Restaurant's Discriminatory Dress Code

A viral video from an ABC news report concerns a recent incident in which a group of Black diners were told they could only sit outside at a New Jersey restaurant because of their casual attire. But the Black diners saw that White arrivals dressed similarly were allowed inside.

The restaurant in question had been in the news because of the same issue two years previously. Unfortunately, a discriminatory incident such as this occurs across the country 24/7. But this video underscores several points.

Diversity in an environment and racism are not mutually exclusive.

Would a 21st-century *Green Book* app have helped? Would the group have visited the restaurant had they known ahead of time of the prior history of dress code discrimination?

Counting on an apology or on a possible boycott after an incident does not repair the stress and humiliation experienced when singled out for poor race-based treatment.

This incident caught my attention because of something the diners tried to do: Report the poor treatment to the security guard. No. That doesn't ever work.

The guard and/or his company works for the restaurant.

Source: Abc7ny.com. Originally published on the Niche Creativity blog in 2021.

Why Two Minority Entrepreneurs Were Arrested at Starbucks

Question: Technology and social movements may help address profiling issues in the consumer marketplace. Recently, for example, cell phone video went viral after the controversial arrest and jailing of two minority men sitting at a Philadelphia Starbuck's.

They were later released without charge. What do you think about this incident and how else might technology put an end to such incidents?

Answer: The term loitering is often defined in vague terms in many jurisdictions. *Black's Law Dictionary* is one example that underscores the issue.

According to witnesses, the two men were sitting quietly for 15 minutes. The Starbucks worker's exchange with the men, prior to calling the police (Nestel), suggests anger was evident. Details in *The Washington Post* provided further clues as to why the situation escalated.

Some might argue that the call to police was racial bias and also a power play.

I would not disagree. The men were later released from jail because Starbucks declined to press charges. One wonders what charges would have applied in this case.

If store owners are concerned with customers who sit for long periods without buying (CNN), then if ordinances permit, management should consider posting at every table a courteous, humorous, and effective policy guideline enforced equally for all people.

Cell phone technology and social media captured and exposed the incident. But Virtual Reality may be an effective tool to educate those who never experience racial bias.

Sources

ABC7News, M.L. Nestel, Handcuffing of 2 Black men in a Starbucks called repressible outcome by CEO. http://abc7.com/handcuffing-of-2-black-men-in-a-starbucks-called-reprehensible-outcome-by-ceo/3344516

ABC7News.com. Comedian, CNN commentator W. Kamau Bell recalls being kicked out of coffee shop. http://abc7news.com/comedian-w-kamau-bell-recalls-being-kicked-out-of-coffee-shop/3351799

WashingtonPost.com, Starbucks to close 8,000 Starbucks for racial bias education. https://www.washingtonpost.com/news/business/wp/2018/04/17/starbucks-to-close-8000-stores-for-racial-bias-education-on-may-29-after-arrest-of-two-black-men.

Money.cnn.com, *GMA* interview. http://money.cnn.com/2018/04/19/news/companies/starbucks-arrests-philadelphia/index.html

NPR.org, The men arrested in Philadelphia Coffeeshop speak out. https://www.npr.org/sections/thetwo-way/2018/04/19/603917872/they-can-t-be-here-for-us-men-arrested-at-philadelphia-starbucks-speak-out

CNN: Eyewitness, This would never happen to me, this doesn't happen to white people, April 16, 2018: https://www.youtube.com/watch?v=JVKZqbzDUl4

Did you know? According to some news reports, one of the two men arrested had been a regular customer at the location since age 15?

Restaurant Discrimination or Bad Service: The Difference

Regardless of race, color, or creed, restaurant diners often experience bad service. Bad customer service is defined in part as customer expectations that are not met. Or what the customer expected was not received.

When a diner believes bad service is discriminatory, other people may not always agree. Bad service may only be an indication of an establishment's chaotic business management.

How bad service is handed out determines the difference between poor service or discrimination. When bad service is directed at everyone, discrimination may not be applicable. But if bad service or treatment is directed toward a specific person or a group of a certain race or ethnicity, the treatment may be discriminatory.

A recent article on Medium by G. Correia revealed his experience when he took his teen son to a specialty restaurant for a hamburger but left after an hours-long wait without being served. "As we left, the chef and the hostess, both unable to hide their exuberance, smiled and waved with giddiness," Correia wrote.

Correia's article includes an overlooked issue for those without firsthand experience: how to act carefully despite bad service to avoid fueling the situation in the presence of a son or daughter. Insightful and infuriating.

While visiting a restaurant with a teen or preteen, I might carry a paperback book to pull out and engage the teen in a quick discussion after encountering questionable service. Is this treatment bad or is it discriminatory? A fill-in checklist for jotting down the restaurant service experience and activities observed would be included. Correia's article inspired me to offer *Restaurant Reviewing* to a general audience.

A parent could ask their son or daughter to write an honest restaurant review of 2-4 sentences about their dining experience and share it on social media. (Without naming the restaurant but giving a general location and food specialty to minimize the risk of being sued).

The paperback journal titled *Restaurant Reviewing: How to understand and write about awful food service in a multi-cultural society* would include local ordinances and state laws for the appropriate region.

And perhaps creating an app or website that collects the positive dining experiences of multicultural diners across the country might be one answer.

Sources

Bad service or no service is part of the Black experience, and inevitable blatant racism doesn't even take a break for a moment so you can enjoy dinner. G Correia, October 23, 2021.

> https://medium.com/illumination-curated/bad-service-or-no-service-is-part-of-the-black-experience-and-inevitable-ccf4cdb23ead

Here is my related article on Medium:

https://medium.com/illumination/restaurant-racism-vs-bad-service-eb7f837b83c7

Combatting racial discrimination in the restaurant industry.

https://www.shegerianlaw.com/combating-racial-discrimination-in-the-restaurant-industry-what-you-should-know-now

Removing customers:

https://www.jdsupra.com/legalnews/removing-customers-when-can-a-texas-res-28991

Food away from home expenditures by race:

https://www.statista.com/statistics/241090/average-us-food-away-from-home-household-expenditures-by-race

State Laws

Civil rights laws guarantee you the right to be treated fairly and without discrimination in all restaurants, stores, and businesses. If you have experienced discrimination, you may file a complaint with the Civil Rights Division of the United States Department of Justice, https://civilrights.justice.gov/

States with laws that provide state relief: California, DC, Florida, Illinois, Michigan, New Jersey, and Pennsylvania.

California Civil Code – The California Unruh Civil Rights Act prohibits discrimination in business on the basis of sex, race, color, religion, ancestry, and disability.

> https://leginfo.legislature.ca.gov/faces/codes_displaySection.xhtml?lawCode=CIV&sectionNum=51

District of Columbia Code – The Washington DC Human Rights Act prohibits direct discrimination on the basis of race, age, religion, and other issues.

> https://code.dccouncil.us/dc/council/code/titles/2/chapters/14

Florida Civil Rights Act of 1992 – *The general purposes of the Florida Civil Rights Act of 1992 are to secure for all individuals within the state freedom from discrimination because of race, color, religion, sex, pregnancy, national origin, age, handicap, or marital status and thereby to protect their interest in personal dignity, to make available to the state their full productive capacities, to secure the state against domestic strife and unrest, to preserve the public safety, health, and general welfare, and to promote the interests, rights, and privileges of individuals within the state.*

http://www.leg.state.fl.us/Statutes/index.cfm?App_mo
de=Display_Statute&URL=0700-0799/0760/0760.html

Illinois Human Rights Act – Freedom from Unlawful
Discrimination. To secure for all individuals within Illinois
the freedom from discrimination against any individual
because of his or her race, color, religion, sex, national
origin, ancestry, age, order of protection status, marital
status, physical or mental disability, military status, sexual
orientation, pregnancy, or unfavorable discharge from
military service in connection with employment, real estate
transactions, access to financial credit, and the availability of
public accommodations.

https://www.ilga.gov/legislation/ilcs/ilcs3.asp?ChapterI
D=64&ActID=2266

Michigan Department of Civil Rights – *MDCR*
investigates complaints to determine whether unlawful
discrimination occurred. While investigating a complaint,
MDCR is impartial and does not act as an advocate or
representative for either party.

https://www.michigan.gov/mdcr/0,4613,7-138-
42240_43561-153171--,00.html

New Jersey Division of Civil Rights – How to File a
Complaint with DCR. Defining "public accommodations" to
include all retail stores and prohibits discrimination in retail
stores and other places of public accommodation based on
race, creed, ethnicity, gender, and sexual orientation).
Claims under the New Jersey statute can be brought under a
disparate treatment or disparate impact theory.

https://www.njoag.gov/about/divisions-and-
offices/division-on-civil-rights-home/division-on-civil-
rights-file-a-complaint

Pennsylvania Human Relations Act

https://www.phrc.pa.gov/Resources/Law-and-Legal/Pages/The-Pennsylvania-Human-Relations-Act.aspx

Consumer Discrimination: The Limitations of Federal Civil Rights Protection, Deseriee A. Kennedy, Touro Law Center. A full-text resource on state and federal laws providing civil rights protections.

https://digitalcommons.tourolaw.edu/cgi/viewcontent.cgi?article=1246&context=scholarlyworks

State public accommodation laws

https://www.ncsl.org/research/civil-and-criminal-justice/state-public-accommodation-laws.aspx

Adapted from *Racial Profiling & Social Justice in the Marketplace*, page 46, by Dee Adams

References

CBS News Black History Month, Feb 9, 2022: Celebrating two trailblazing chefs Alexander Smalls and Kwame Onwuachi.

https://www.cbsnews.com/video/a-conversation-with-two-trailblazing-chefs-on-carving-their-own-culinary-paths

Black Secret Service agents sue Denny's. Six black Secret Service agents filed a federal lawsuit Monday against Denny's restaurant chain.

https://www.upi.com

Racial Segregation - Restaurant-ing through history.

https://restaurant-ingthroughhistory.com

In November, 1961, new Interstate Commerce Commission (ICC) rules took effect requiring all interstate bus terminals.

https://restaurant-ingthroughhistory.com

Blacks, not whites, told to pay before dining. Now Federal Way Denny's workers are jobless.

https://www.newstribune.com

Employees at a Federal Way Denny's no longer are employed at the restaurant after the chain investigated an allegedly

https://www.thenewstribune.com

Restaurant's Right to Refuse Service Law

https://www.legalmatch.com

Restaurant's Right to Refuse Service Law: Customer service isn't the easiest aspect of running a restaurant. There may be times when you need to refuse service.

https://www.legalmatch.com

Ending Discrimination at America's Diner, Denny's Restaurant is known as "America's diner." But in the early 1990s, the Washington Lawyers' Committee exposed it.

https://www.washlaw.org

Insuron.com blog, Can you legally refuse to serve your customers?

https://www.insureon.com/blog/can-you-legally-refuse-to-serve-your-customers

Funny account of nightmare dining at an upscale eatery: language, Medium.com

https://medium.com/@everywhereist/bros-lecce-we-eat-at-the-worst-michelin-starred-restaurant-ever-3466c98cdbdf

About the Author

Dee Adams is the author of *Racial Profiling & Social Justice in the Marketplace: An inside look at what you should know but probably do not know about shopping and racial profiling.*

For other titles, check out her ad-free multicultural blog: https://nichecreativity.com/racial-profiling-and-social-justice-blog.

www.ingramcontent.com/pod-product-compliance
Lightning Source LLC
Chambersburg PA
CBHW030300030426
42336CB00009B/457